Tears of a King

John Hypocrace Lewis

PenFire Publishing
Kansas City, MO
penfirepublishing.com

Copyright © 2023 by John Hypocrace Lewis
All rights reserved. No part of this book may be reproduced, scanned, or distributed in any printed or electronic form, including information storage and retrieval systems, without permission. Please do not participate in or encourage piracy of copyrighted materials in violation of the author's rights. Please purchase only authorized editions.
First Edition: December 2023
ISBN: 978-1-952838-13-2
This book is a work of fiction. Names, characters, places, dates, and incidents are products of the author's imagination or are used fictitiously, satirically, or as parody. Any resemblance to actual persons, living or dead, business establishments, events, or locales is entirely coincidental.
10 9 8 7 7 5 4 3 3 1
Design, Layout, Edits: Sheri Hall

Table of Contents

One. 8

Two. 10

Three. 13

Four. 15

Five. 17

Six. 19

Seven. 20

Eight. 21

Nine. 23

Ten. 25

Eleven. 27

Twelve. 29

Thirteen. 31

Fourteen. 33

Fifteen. 35

Sixteen. 36

Seventeen. 37

Eighteen. 39

Nineteen. 40

Twenty. 42

Twenty-One. 45

Bio. 48

One.

It's said that   God is agape.
Meaning   God is love.
To know love
           is
               To know God.
               God has no form.
Meaning   Love has no form,
               No one set version.

My encounters with love have been a battle, and I hate fighting God. I bare-knuckle brawl with my life in the palm of my hand, with beating hearts as the war drum. It's tribal—a gift given and often mishandled.

        I don't know exactly what love is.
        Does that mean I don't know God?

Is my relationship with God so shaky that one on this plane isn't in the picture? A wonder painted before my years with colors unseen. A creation created from my rib.

Am I so much of a broken thing that I don't know when someone is trying to love me? Why can't I see the God in them; Know I'm worthy? I share the love in me till it's draining. I no longer search for the God in people. We all have a side-eye view of love.

God, I love you wholeheartedly.
But why can't I love another?
I wonder if they see the God in me. Meaning do they know I'm capable of love, too?

My reflection begins to morph. I don't know what to do.

Like really?
The spirit in me says fight. But my flesh-like mind says

            Fuck it!!
          You trapped in me.

We tapped in niggah.
What God can you call and talk to?
Don't no God live here in this labyrinth you call a mind!
You don't know what love is.
All you know is arms' length.
Lucifer, false god, light bringer, was tossed out.
He was loved the most!
Look what happened to him!
And look what I did to you.

Twisting slide, downward spiral,
look how lost you are, boy.
Where is the Peter Pan you wrote about?
Your love's Ten Commandments?
It's only Wendy 'cause you sleep alone now.
You really alone now.
Only love can save you.
The real question is,
do you see the God in yourself?

I can't argue with reflection.
It's too much like talking to self.
But ain't that prayer,
Conversation hoping love hears you?
I mean, God, are you listening?
I understand the message loud and clear.

I need to love myself before I love others.

John, I love you wholeheartedly.

Two.

Doc, I did what you suggested: the poem to my depression.
I wrote it, and the exercise exorcised a few hidden demons.

Exercise I

You make up one part of me
I worry about you
I mean
Us

I feel like we
      In Arkham Asylum

FINDING
      Comfort in dark rooms
           With white dusty walls
      Peace in dripping
         Leaking
         Soaking in sorrow

That's not me.
You seem to like company
This is crippling
Bed becomes a dark, sinking place
Making blankets the only hugs
We look forward to
              Safe, warm
But still in this asylum
A place I once held as my sanctuary
My Mind
Flooded with a barrage of questions

RIDDLE ME THIS!
Does she even like me?
Why am I so broken?
Do I attract broken things?
Is that why I'm always alone?

I don't think you realize
You've stolen sleep from me

Had me wide awake
Till the sun peaks
Making people ask

        Are you okay?
        What's going on?
        You too silent, and your light is dim!
        Why you so Dark Knight gloomy?
        You funny,
        Batman who laughs!

I don't know
How to answer
Their questions
Dr. Quinn
I can't answer
The ones I have

I know Anxiety is working
With you Depression
Yall are a tag team
I'm wrestling while restless
Opponents sheets and pillows
Penguin and Mr. Freeze
Doing my damndest not to
Get frozen to the mat-tress

So now I give part truths

        Kicking out   Grabbing the ropes

          Speaking in code

"I'm ok."

"I can't complain."

    MEANS

        "Help me!"

        "I'm just trying to make it to tomorrow,
        and
          the tomorrows after."

Exercise II

Depression,

You turned my smile into a mask. Why so serious? I can't stand being serious! Now, I'm a Joker, I'm always putting on a show. Like, I'm killing it! Depression, why you got so many faces? I thought I was bipolar how my attitude would switch, Two Face, no, Harvey Dent. Now, I'm the reflection of my broken self. Even when I'm not the problem it's a switch in me to apologize, try to mend. I wonder is that's a newly added toxic trait nicely tucked away in this clay man.

There's those depressing assed questions! Change face I'm Scarecrow, formally Dr. I tried to heal myself, but I was hallucinating in this asylum, ready for a fight I created myself. Mad hatter in a world I created with no Alice or Cat Woman to be seen. I fight 'cause I don't want depression to Bane me, backbreaking after a flex. I turned detective to get to the bottom of my triggers. To make my fight as strong as Commissioner Gordon's will. So, when I look at the man in the mirror this time, I'm acknowledging you.

And if you show yo depressing ass face, I will fuck you up.
'Cause I'm Batman.

Three.

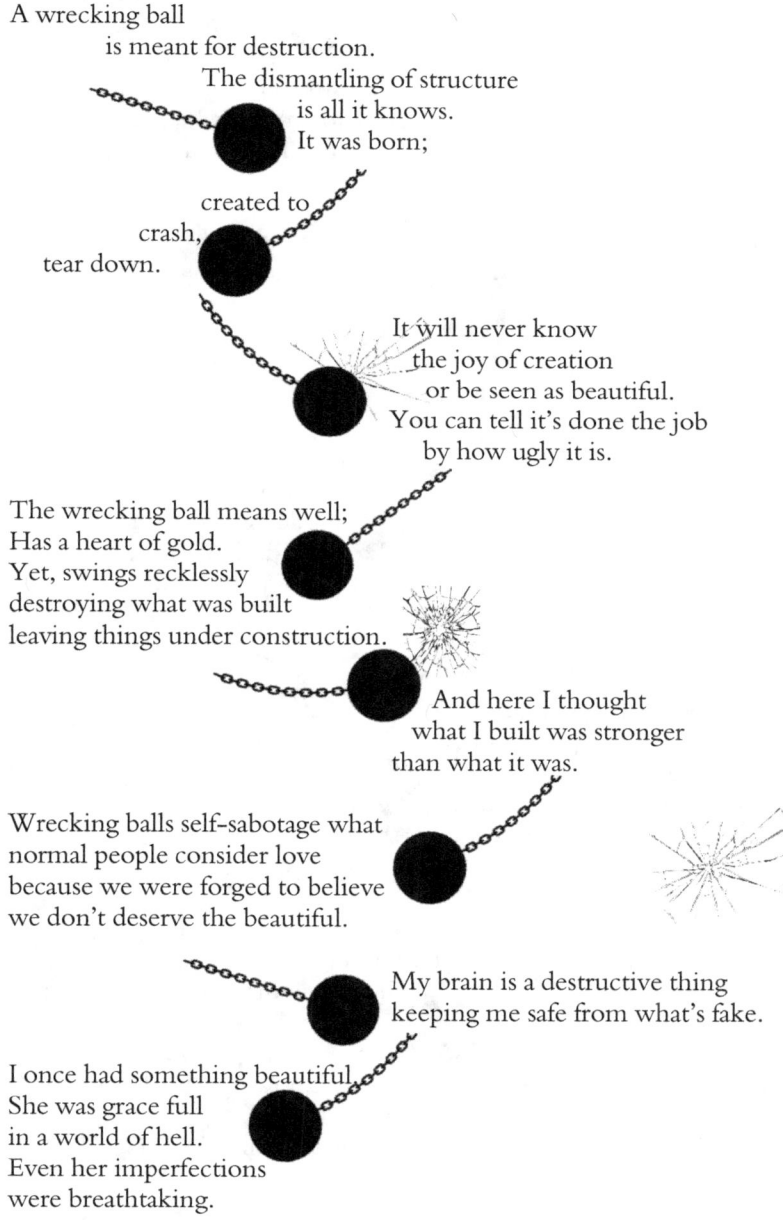

A wrecking ball
    is meant for destruction.
        The dismantling of structure
          is all it knows.
          It was born;

    created to
  crash,
tear down.

        It will never know
        the joy of creation
         or be seen as beautiful.
        You can tell it's done the job
         by how ugly it is.

The wrecking ball means well;
Has a heart of gold.
Yet, swings recklessly
destroying what was built
leaving things under construction.

      And here I thought
       what I built was stronger
       than what it was.

Wrecking balls self-sabotage what
normal people consider love
because we were forged to believe
we don't deserve the beautiful.

      My brain is a destructive thing
       keeping me safe from what's fake.

I once had something beautiful.
She was grace full
in a world of hell.
Even her imperfections
were breathtaking.

She said I was handsome.
I said   *Me?*
         How could something
         built for destruction
         be handsome?
Destroyed the compliment
Before it could build a
foundation…and left.

She was a fighter.
she beat my objections,
she beat her nemesis,
she beat cancer,
she beat beat beat
the thought of love
from my lips.

   Torturing me while
    cracking a smile.
     Made me the joker
      in a deck of cards;
      I fooled myself! Simp.
      You were … *happy.*

The truth, too painful to believe.
She led me by a string.
Me, a swinging puppet marionette
of a wrecking ball.
No new plans for structures.
Just the construction site of
a relationship in ruins.

    I'll be the villain in your story.
     I'll admit that I smashed repeatedly.
      I'll pretend there were no feelings.
      Tell them I destroyed your peace.
      Leave out how you wounded me,
   used me, not knowing what I was built for.

Not knowing how much of a wreck I really am.

Four.

pro·gram·ming /ˈprōˌgramiNG/
noun
1. The process of making a set of instructions to a computer that tells it how to perform a task.

Me /mē,mi/
noun
1. A human child.
2. A young novice with only the set of instructions that came from my parents.

She /SHē/
noun
1. An expert programmer.
2. A babysitter.

I was too young to know better
Common sense wasn't developed
Naïve   I was easy to manipulate
She taught me her code
Played with me in empty rooms
Making secret bathroom trips
To give lessons on anatomy
Strange reciprocity   Conditional statements
If I do this   You do that
Had me suckle her nipple
To repay her
After she sucked me
Felt the tingle in my bones
But I wasn't yet able to release
Couldn't give her the gift
She should've received
I wasn't even prepubescent
It wasn't developed
When I sucked her nipple
It reminded me of home
Of mother's milk
But they were bare
No nutrition from
That Amazonian temptress

15

Just corruption in my system
Coding early sexuality
Just hand   Caressing head
As if to say   You're doing well
                             I've taught you well

I thought it was normal
Active at an early age
                             I didn't ask for it

But with great power
Comes an array of responsibility
I've kept the secret that lingers
In the shadow of pride
I made myself feel like
I was a man early
Programmed myself to believe
I wasn't molested   Nah I wasn't molested
I was trained   Trained well
                             Is it still molestation
                             If it was a woman?
                             If it felt good
                             If she was nice
                             If she coded me to
                             Make women feel nice
I'm just going on the lessons
I was taught
                             I was taught it wasn't wrong.
I was broken even before
I understood I was broken.
Had to take a glimpse at my past
And every time I look
The programming reappears
Us in an empty room!
Us in an empty room!
Us in an empty room!
I'm just now acknowledging it
Coming to the realization that
                             It happens
                             It happened to me
I know now   It's not a badge of honor

Five.

One of my favorite stories
Is the emperor's new clothes
I dare you to tell this king
He don't look good
I wear these items
    Or lack thereof
With the confidence of royalty
I enjoy clothes
    Ohhhh and shoes!
I never leave home without 'em
I always try to look
Fly   Flashy   Fancy with my selections
Bound to get a complement
I'm fresh
    Dressed like a million bucks

My depression
Resembles a denim vest
With rusted nails sticking out of seams
From its tack like decor
    But I wear it well
It's bothersome
It resembles camouflage
Blends in
It's the shadow of my shadow
Lighter than the original
    Who pays attention to that?
You say I'm strong
Stunned at how I keep my head up
Ain't no making this king bow
Smiling even in battle
I've fought for so long
I didn't realize it looked like
Fighting brought me joy

My depression be the flyest kicks
I'm a sneakerhead always in my head
Wondering if they will focus on my feet
Or ask me how I be
But I be losing sleep

Can't shed a tear
Over spilled milk
I crack a joke
Something to distract
From the real question at hand
>   *Where you get your shoes from?*
>   *These old things,*
>   *I keep 'em clean tho.*
Who wants to wear dirty depression
They look good but still beat
There is no retreat

The daredevil in me says chance it
Put depression on in plain site
>   *Who's gon see past the façade;*
Then someone looks in my eyes
Asks if I'm alright
And like the Berlin Wall
Once strong and dividing
I crumble into a dust like cloud
With a river of tears on the inside

Outside I portray ease
Corked bottle closed off and silent
Fixing my vest
Now heavier than before
I utter
>   *I'm alive.*
>   *I can't complain.*
I sound robotic
My depression looks good to you
But takes a lot out of me
Bet not step on my kicks
Or talk about my silence
I think you'll see the imposter in me

Cause even king's ask
>   *Do I look good today?*

Six.

We haven't talked in a while.

For that, I apologize. I hope you understand. It wasn't intended, just felt a disconnect. I mean, you were gone when I really needed you.

I, rock bottom, having conversations with gravel. Rock be best friend, should've been you. But you haven't spoke to me. I mean, two wrongs don't make a right. I know. You can only wait and listen for so long. Then you're stagnant with no out. You said you would provide an out; nothing is too much for me to handle. But this? It was. Why put her in my path without warning me that THIS Eve wasn't from MY rib? She was the snake that led man to damnation on Earth.

She didn't hold good intent. Tasted good like the apple, too good to be true. She wasn't the completion of my circle: false love, false prophet.

I don't blame you. The flesh played a part, a big part. But you could have stopped it from the start instead of letting me be entertained by smoke and mirrors, not knowing it was my spirit burning.

She tried to destroy my temple. You know, flip tables. It wasn't like I was selling something in yo name, birth from Agape.

I'm not placing blame; I'm just hoping for guidance and trying to find a wife in this hell on Earth.

A peace of mind.
A lil peace of heaven.
A light in a dark world.

'Cause "When a man finds a wife he finds a good thing."
And I want a good thing. I mean, doesn't your son deserve a good thing?

Seven.

A word, as you descend in your darkened place …

I know what the straw looks like that broke the camel's back; the last string pulled to make this puppet dance, entertain. I know what it's like for all the tabloids to print what a villain looks like. In my case, it looks green-shaded. You seem to blend so well with your envy. My first memory wasn't a sweet one. I learned what hate was before I knew the warm embrace of hugs. I know what a cold shoulder feels like.

I wonder, did you get hugs? Were you loved? Did you smile? Didn't you live in a two-parent home with family pictures hanging?

I was adopted, lost, and found. I was stumbled upon and raised by womxn. They didn't understand, but I didn't think to take it *that* far.

Who took the time to understand you before you became a grim reaper carrying modern-day sickle leaving bullet points and hitting targets? What was the trigger that made you, pull the trigger without a warning; the unseen signs prior to the massacre? There had to be signs, written messages hidden in sketches with vivid detail.

You had 1000 words but spoke none before you crossed the line.

How did you respond to the screams of children?
Did it remind you how you felt on the inside?
You ain't much older than them.
What's the message you wanted to send?

Eight.

Where I live
Zombies lurk
Posted up on corners
This horde
A class of human
Seen but not heard
Silent walkers
To us
Speaking in zombie tongue
With each other
An intelligent
Meeting of the minds
Lucid vision swirl

    How did they end up like this?

Laughing
A husk of a human
Fueled with morning showers
Of Seagram's gin
Pores seeping from last night's
Home Sweet Home vodka episode
In search of the next fix
Nose is too expensive
Next best thing is cooked
Street pharmacists
Supply hits
We question the trip
They first class elitists
With frequent flyer miles
Sky high

I avoid them
To not get exposed
To their contagion
But who am I to judge
I'm a fractured being
Hoping to mend
The broken in me

Having more in common
With them than with someone
who has it *under control*

Me
Silently walking
Lashing weaponized tongue
Infecting myself more
Chemical change
I'm shifting
Transforming
Into what I attempted to avoid
I wonder if there is a cure
For the toxic in me
I guess it begins with
Acknowledgement
And asking those close
To understand
Help me learn
Listen
And not keep me at arm's length
Avoiding me like plague

Nine.

Oh
How I miss the days of old

The 90s
When disposable cameras
Ruled the world
Take a chance
Get a good angle
Wind up till the click
If it don't sound like
Iron Man's hand beam
You won't have a flash
 Picture be darker than normal
       Cousin Tammy is light-skinned!
       Why she look so Wesley Snipes?!
       You forgot the flash!

The 90s is how it was meant
To capture a moment
While being in the moment
The outdoor sky
Natural light
Open field background
Memories that will last a lifetime
18-24 moments locked in a box
Waiting to be released
Where 6 or maybe even all
Have red eyes

Disposable cameras held secrets
And the more you had
The more risk
Playing Russian Roulette with images
    Is this my wife's home lingerie photoshoot
    Or an important family function?
You won't know till it's developed

From birthday parties to graduations
You didn't move until the very last
Klink of fingers pressing a button

Quick Draw McGraw
May even get two
And it's always an aunt
Who forgets she brought hers
Deep in the cave of her purse
Pockets and section's divided
You love her
         So you wait
It was precious time spent
Snails paced and relaxed

We got away from this
Moments fill now the cloud
Holding selfies and usies
Cell phones
Equipped with front-facing flashes
And auto light adjustment
Preventing dark images and red eyes

We are now fast-paced streamers
Point and post
Snap Chatting
Instagram plastering
Twitter X feeders
Filling Facebook
For all to know

We don't live life firsthand anymore
We watch others live it
    Where's the reel?
    Man, last night looked lit!
We don't live in moments anymore
If it didn't get posted
You didn't have that experience
    Where's the real?
    No disposable camera
    waiting in eager anticipation
    of what was once
    a tangible souvenir.

Ten.

Hi, I'm Hypocrace.

I mean, I'm John.

Hi, I'm John, and you probably don't want to hear this poem about me. A glimpse into things I noticed but hide well from you. Bet you didn't know I hid behind laughter for a year once, it was the only duct tape I could find.

My shell was cracked. I got a chink in my armor, that's why I don't fight this battle. Life is not safe. It's draining, killing my happy, and making me monster. Ink is my only escape. I talk to paper.

I talk to paper more than I do people. Call it therapy and myself artist. When really, I'm lonely in a room full of hearts beating like mine. Scared to die and not be loved. But I guess that means I'm alive. To feel fear, pain, regret. Still using laughter as duct tape, bandage.

Broke a cardinal sin. I wasted time, something I can never get back, on dead-end journeys that lead to blockades. A road full of land mines, infatuated. Making dessert out of salty things. Always got the bitter, never the sweet.

My last smile, my last *real* smile (Not the mask I wear to make people comfortable.), was in my youth. When laughing was just that. Cares were free, and streetlight was curfew. It's been too long, and forcing this mask hurts. The muscles just don't move the same, ain't used 'em in a while. What do I have to smile about?

I'm an introvert with extrovert tendencies, a two-sided coin. You never know what you going to get, 50/50 split.

Heads: I'm the center of attention. Hell, I'm a gas to be around! People love my energy and how well I feed souls. Even when mine is in shambles, think I was a medic in my past life. I mean, I must've been for as well as I can bandage a wound, make it presentable, believable that I'm okay.

I once hid behind laughter for a year, it was the only bandage I could find strong enough to keep me from breaking. Piled up the chipped pieces of my soul and puzzled together a new body.

I rarely flip tails: Back of the line. Vibe in my own world. Surrounded but solo and content with just being. Knowing being is enough. Knowing you don't have to feed souls when you're famished. It's not selfish to recharge, no matter how much time it takes. Can't rush 100%. A watched pot don't boil; it will take a while for the new body to mend.

I once held in my problems for a year, hid them behind laughter. Called it healing.

Eleven.

The Dark Ages
5th – 14th century
For 900 years
Nothing emerged
No new art recorded
After its passing
A new age was born
The Age of Enlightenment
This sounds familiar

I've been doing poetry
For a decade-plus
My darkest point
Was in the seventh
That one year felt like 100
In my dark age
No new work emerged
My pen eluded me
Mind was dry

Might as well
Skip to the end
Can't worry about life
Without life
My mind is a battlefield

In the Dark Age
There were ups and downs
Dark times
Trial by fire
And in learning this
I understood the crowd wouldn't
Always love me
I stayed strong and
Didn't downplay my gifts

Now enlightened
I've witnessed shocking truths
Soft as whispers
Can barely hear the pain

In the poem
I was told I don't sound authentic
As if the words
And thoughts weren't mine

I was assumed incapable
As if my hard-shell
And the blackness of my speech
Is too much to connect
With brokenness crowds swoon for

I don't do it for scores
But four scores
And few years back
I wanted to evolve
Transform
Into a being
Not like myself
And almost lost myself
Poetry found me again

My survival is authentic
Trying to open my secrets
Kept me in the sunken place
Tapped the cup
Sending me to my plummet
Puppet poet doing the jig
You strung me to do
I won't let my darkness consume me
Won't allow it to make me hate poetry

Twelve.

To the womxn that turned down my advances due to my height
~Or~
To say I'd be better if my personality were in a taller vessel

I'm trying to find a catchy title
To a big assed elephant in the room

To those who would say
If height makes the man
I'm less of one
'Cause I'm not tall
Bravo to you for having power
over the uncontrollable!
I know we all have *preferences*
But
Am I not tall enough to find a good thing?

If I check all the boxes
You complain about
Fall for my personality
      Which is my spirit
I was made in His image
You can't say I'm not
I honestly have no control

Origin story
My mother is 4' 9"
The end
That's it
Fin
Fanito
I'm working with what I got

Vertically
      I'm challenged
Horizontally
      I'm not
      I'm above average
I'm Black MacGyver
Making bombs out of foil

Gum and a rubber band
I make a way out of nothing
Me being short
Don't make my love smaller

Yet you find a taller man
Who's an asshole
'Cause he knows he's tall
Justifying his verbal assaults
Mental beatings and physical wounds

Being tall doesn't keep him at home
As he roams as Romans do
Living single when not in your presence
Having babies with other womxn
Making you stepmom

Question
How tall must one be
To turn a house into a home
If height makes the man
Then age ain't got shit to do with it
A heart in a short man
Isn't big enough for two
Only space enough for one
      Right?
      Really?
Is my height that much of a dealbreaker?
You wish to destroy the temple
I opened for you
'Cause I opened up to you
Turning personal trials
Group session conversations
Then picking a man of lesser character
Because of their height

                            Wait, I'm trying to find a title…

    To the womxn that turned down my advances due to my height,
                            Thank you!

Thirteen.

Acrophobia
> Fear of heights

Aerophobia
> Fear of flying

We know

Arachnophobia
> Fear of spiders

Astraphobia
> Fear of thunder and lightning

Autophobia
> Fear of being alone

Or

Anuptaphobia
> Fear of staying single

Alone
As in with one's self
Succumbing to thoughts
Unable to escape the mind
It's a trap
I seem to find parts
Of myself in these

It's interesting
Some of these fit snug
Like a too-small sweater
We all have small fears
That we see as huge

Gamophobia
> Fear of marriage

Gynophobia
> Fear of women

Philophobia
> Fear of love

I find it hard

To say I love you
To things that are
Forever fleeting
Never truly loved a womxn
Other than family
I love beautiful sunlit days
And crisp moonlit nights

I've noticed
None of my siblings
Have significant others
How hard it is to trust
It makes me sad
Makes me howl at the moon
On clear sky nights

Believe me
I've tried to find it
I searched and realized
You don't search
It finds you

I wouldn't say my fear
Of womxn is a phobia
It's still a fear none-the-less
And I be a fool
Sending an S O S
Hoping to get bit
By the love bug
Or hit with Cupid's arrow
In my hopeless romantic heart
Hidden deep under calloused flesh
Beating Morse code
Sending a signal saying
.. / .-- .- -. - / - --- / .-.. --- ...- . / -.-- --- ..- --..-- / .--. ..... --- -.... .. .-
... / .- -. -.. / .- .-.. .-.. .-.-.-
"I want to love you, phobias and all."

Fourteen.

she stole my heart
like candy from a baby
easy
she leads me
on a journey
to find her's
she's smart
but love is an art
i was just hoping
i could reach
number one on her chart
so i set sail
captain jack as my lead
his compass will
take me to her
she is my wendy
i am her pan
but i'm a grown man
i put childish things away
only things i play
are video games at times
phase 10 or dominos
so keep in mind
i don't like games
so let this fairy tail
be on the same page
the same stage too
we need to think alike
so i write

These are my loves 10 commandments.
1. Communication is key.
2. You are all I need.
3. I wake up to hear you speak.
4. My life now is an open door.
5. This is my favorite chapter.
6. And the one after cause you're in it.
7. If I die I'll wait for you in heaven.
8. You are the wind.
9. I don't need to pretend.

10. I love your face.

your smile brightens my day
and when you're sad
the world cries
let me dry your eyes
and rock you to sleep
take away your bad dreams
and replace them
with images of me
you make me blush
you have the forbidden stuff
i want to get close to you
breathe when you breathe
leave when you leave
so allow me
to follow this blueprint
give you this gift
1-10 are about you
the angel God sent

Fifteen.

Call me Indiana Jones!

With a leather hat, a whip, and an array of helping hands. I search in places unseen, deep in caves, history frozen. Time still moves, but love, love is something I thought I found.

I lost my hat trying to save her. I wanted to save her, but she was beyond saving. She was lost from jump, and the fall didn't kill her. I just wanted to find her. I was emergency rescue. This is the dream I had.

I slept a year while continuing a daily routine, draining my life force. I was sucked in. Not chasing love, chasing attention. We lost ours. No bad intentions just grew further apart. Lies will do that.

Have you ever held a heart beating? It was once in sync, but as distance grew, it lost its connection. Flatline. The feeling's similar to death.

So, I built a fence. It protected my perimeter as my heart battled. I made a decision never to let my heart battle again. War isn't for me. Love isn't war.

I'd be lying if I said I believed that.

That's like saying I ain't scared of nothing when I'm deathly afraid of snakes and dying alone.

I'm alone now. Who knows when my time's up? Hands up!
Don't rush it! Don't look Indiana Jones! Certain caves aren't meant to be searched by man. Who knows what you will rustle loose.

My dreams and reality are beginning to be the same. Caves once searched are women once lost. I wish I had never searched certain caves.

I'd be lying if I said I believed that.

Sixteen.

I

three steps in/the furthest i've been/quick to befriend enemies hidden/my life is a war behind enemy lines/physically i'm fine/but my mind/shambles/like eggs/scrambled/heart ripped from flesh/i'm worse than the walking dead/even then my mind would be gone/i'm walking heartless/"How can I hurt you?"/mind and spirit trying to make a truce/but a broken heart/a bitter flesh won't let it come true/can't feel blue/that bonds us/so i'm locked in bondage/i'm a hostage/my mind is holding my soul for ransom

II

I know this is random,
but have you seen the sky today?
It's kinda grey,
which is better than yesterday.
The sky was pitch black,
as if it was night all day.
Safe to say, I like grey.
The clouds are moving
and letting in light.
It's nice.
It feels right.
I'm in a happy median,
living life at medium.
High on hopes weighing pros.
Spitting sentences that
can heal gashes and holes.

But a genuine broken heart,
I can't fix those.
So, I unload, reload,
jot down, catch up,
find the flow,
just let it blow.
Let loose my rage on a page.
Kill what you used to be
and replace it with
what I see today,
                Grey.

Seventeen.

Fact
History ain't nothing
But a written memory
Passed down for others
To study
To learn from
To not make the same
Choices in the future
To say
You won't make
The same mistake twice

I have yet to learn the lesson
I still give energy
To things that won't hold life

If relationships are gardens
I overfeed dead things
My green thumb is a
Black thumb of death
No flowers bloom
To make beautiful bouquets
The good I see in others
Eventually dies in my hands
I've wasted sentences
And attention
Talking to dead rose buds
That never blossomed
Tulips are all I get
I'm used to sex and leave
Fall off like autumn leaves

I'm a Dandelion to myself
I'm ok with this
I'll stick to weeds
Or annuals needing
To be planted yearly
Things can change
At the snap of a season
Perennials come and go

Live long and prosperous
There is no we
Came up short
I can't even grow wheat
I need sunflowers
I think I'm radio-active
That's why I don't get further
Than a strong stem
And root gripping

It's hard to pull these
Dead things up
And as a poet
I make it sound so pretty
Like the grass is greener
On this side
When all I write about
Is the failure
Saying I won't make
The same mistake
This time
Next time
Three times
Maybe four
I'm so used to it
It's normal
Which makes me regret
The attempt
To garden

Eighteen.

The words
I   love   you
Don't slip past
My lips lightly
It's like lighting
Never in the
Same spot twice
Leaving loved ones
Shocked
Electrified
Stuck
Wondering
     Is the end?
     Did hell freeze over?
     Is bacon soaring
     Like twister cows?
I want to evolve
Into one that uses
Words of affirmation
I use actions
They speak louder
When she says
     I love you.
I don't know
How to respond
Being a mirror
Is the hardest thing
For this human to be
Repeat
I am not a copycat
Love outside of family
Ain't in my life
How can I love you
I haven't learned
To love myself
I just talk a good game
Using confident sentences
To camouflage insecurity

Nineteen.

It's said,
> *Not all heroes wear capes.*

Heroes don't do it for acknowledgment, they just want to assist their fellow man. Sometimes preventing them from harming themselves.

To be human
Is to be fragile and strong
Equally balanced
Normal
It's also said
You're only as strong
As your weakest link

I can't fly but
When I saw you
On the ledge
Ready to jump
I found a cape
Dusted it off
Embodied Superman

Shazam
Transformed from Billy
With the capability
To soar
Faster than a speeding bullet
I spoke
And you heard

> *Paused*

I was able to take action
Swift
Didn't talk you off the ledge
But you could trust me
I was Blank Man
And Other Guy
With an old sheet cape

Saw the solo hot and ready
Quivering as much as you
The bullet jumped from the ledge
Volunteering itself as tribute
Not wanting to take the life
It was asked to meet
It knew it was too soon

I was as powerless
As Batman
Robin
But somehow
I was able to disarm
Without bodily harm
This wasn't the end for you

>   You said
> *I wouldn't be here if it wasn't for you.*
>   I thought
> *I wouldn't have forgiven myself if you did it.*

Not all hero's wear capes
And they don't do it
For acknowledgment
But when you asked for help
That's when you became
A hero
In your own right

Missouri has the 10th-highest rate of gun suicides and gun suicide attempts in the US. An average of 673 people in Missouri die from gun suicides. 68 are wounded by gun suicide attempts every year.

You don't have to be a hero to listen.

Twenty.

The heart
A pumping muscle
An engine
Keeping the body moving
Working
Blood flowing like oil
With many connections
The engine works alongside
The computer
Making gears shift
Cogs turn
Joints bend

The ~~brain~~ computer
Communicates with
The ~~body~~ engine
Telling it how to move
Both equally important

I realize my brain and heart
Have never been on
The same wavelength
My heart makes decisions
Emotional
My brain is cut and dry
Logical
My spirit
Broken
I don't have normal reactions
I've learned not to
Follow my heart
That path leads to
Dented appliances
A fridge took the brunt
Of heartfelt pain
Rage

When my grandmother died
I received the call
My engine seized

Locked
Made my computer crash
I was unable to process

When I got the call
Time was irrelevant
Sound muted around
I had control of the chaos
But not enough to give
Her new life to the one who
Lived for 98 years and left
On her terms

There was an explosion
From the engine
My knees buckled
Floating in mid-air
For what seemed like a lifetime
I found myself in a chair
Unaware how I got there
My rebellious brain tried
It's hardest to protect my heart
And my pressurized heart attacked
I'm pounding my head
As if it's the fridge
To bare-knuckle brawl with tears
Because I am still in public
My ~~computer~~ brain overexerted itself
Clocking in overtime
Calculating
Aching bones cracking
Under pressure
Can't adjust to this new existence
Where my grandmother will never
Give me another answer
For questions about life

And to this day
I have yet to process
Any of this

Letting my ~~computer~~ brain
Keep me busy

So I have no time
To sit and fester
In a blue screen of death

I'll miss her.
I lost a part of my ~~engine~~ heart
Only holding on to memories
Saved on this hard drive

Twenty-One.

I've come to the general conclusion that I am, and possibly will be, for an extended period of time, a permanent member of,

THE *FRIEND* ZONE

And I'm ok with this,

I *GUESS*.

You know, having regular conversations and shit, and when the question just so happens to arise (and we know it will), I know how to answer. Been saying it for years; call it practice.

WE *JUST* FRIENDS.

As I clench teeth, eyes big in disbelief. Like, REALLY! Had the thought even crossed your mind? Like forgetting to dot an I, we're like two peas in a pod. It's human nature to grow, and like a Chinese bamboo tree, I want to grow. I'll wait 5yrs before I even start to show. But I'll never give up, forever planting a seed and such. You know we meant to be together; we stuck together through the bad weather, so this journey is nothing.

I want to see you happy with a real smile, like the ones I give you after frowns. Or when you tellin' me, "He ain't shit! It's time to call it quits!" And I'm like, "Think on it now."

But honestly, what I want to say is:

Drop everything, come quick!
You in trouble!
Don't call on Tyrone, call me!

I'm	Heartbeat, waiting to skip a beat When you enter the room.
I'm	The gasp of air taken before loss of breath. When you sneeze
I'm	Sending prayers to protect. Or just randomly speaking your name.

So, I'll be *FRIENDS* till the end of time. It's good we are friends first, takes time to build a bond unbroken in space. But know, our hearts sing the most beautiful melody illuminating those around. It's infectious, like the smile after a compliment or me just seeing your face. But I'll never speak. Don't want to tarnish thoughts of what we have 'cause it's important to me.

So, friend? Yeah, I'm cool being in that zone. It's like home. Just know, you've got space available to occupy in my mind and heart 'cause I see wife in you.

And ain't that best friend first?

Bio

John "Hypocrace" Lewis, "your favorite poet's favorite poet," has been in the poetry community for 10+ years. He represented Kansas City along with his team "FTW" on a national poetry slam level in 2015, 17, and 18. He is the current slam master of "The Regulators," ranked 5th in the Midwest region 16th in the southern region, the host of I am Hypocrace presents: Third Thursday's during poetry on the vine paying artist to feature, slam or cypher. He is the creator of Spoken Easy, a prohibition-style open mic.

He has become a crowd favorite at the local open mic "Soul Sessions" held on Mondays at the Kc Juke House on the historic 18th and Vine, gaining him acknowledgment from media outlets such as 41 Action News and 38 the spot as well as being a featured poet in the month of April 2018 by the Music and More Foundation. His hard work and love of the craft doesn't go unnoticed, as he was nominated in the Kansas City Poetry Awards for both Poet of the Year and Best Slam Poet 2018. 2021/22 and a 2022 finalist for the Best Male Spoken Word Artist Award from the National Spoken Word Awards. He was a 2021/22 finalist for the Kansas City People Choice Awards (top 5), winning the 2022 award and Sponsored Artist of the Year for Poetry for Personal Power. He hopes to learn more as he engages more audiences and further builds his brand ˈpoʊətri.

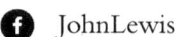 JohnLewis

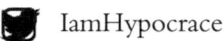 IamHypocrace